Thirty

From Washing Dishes to Wall Street
My Journey Pursuing the American Dream

Thirty-One Dollars

From Washing Dishes to Wall Street
My Journey Pursuing the American Dream

By Mahmoud ElAwadi
and
Debbie Viguié

Published by Mount Sinai

Thirty-One Dollars: From Washing Dishes to Wall Street
My Journey Pursuing the American Dream

ISBN-13: 978-0-692-19415-7

Published by Mount Sinai

Dedicated to my dad, may his soul rest in peace, who gave all his life to raise me to be the man I am today, and to America, the land of the free and the home of the brave.

Acknowledgments

There are a number of people I need to thank without whom this book and, indeed, my American journey would not have been possible. I need to thank my parents. My dad made me the man I am today. My mom taught me never to give up on my dream and to work harder every day to be who I want to be. A huge thank you to my son who is my hero and the main reason why the USA is my home. To my wife who was there for me in the darkest moments, without your support it would have been much harder to keep our family together. Thank you for everything you do. Thank you to my fellow Americans who welcomed me and took me as one of them, I will forever be grateful. To Egypt, the first civilization where I obtained my education and learned the skills that helped me achieve the American dream, I owe a debt of gratitude. To all who helped me on my journey thank you, I will never forget the part you played in getting me this far.

-M.E.

Thank you as always to my husband, Scott, and my parents for their constant support and encouragement. Thank you, Mood, for inviting me on this crazy journey. Thank you to Marim, his lovely, gracious, and very funny wife, for making me laugh.

-D.V.

My father, my son, and me

1
America Calling

My American journey began on September 11, 2001. I will never forget the horror I felt watching the news broadcast showing the World Trade Center Towers collapsing. Over and over the newscaster kept shouting that America had been hit. People were shocked, crying. I stood there, dumbfounded, surrounded by so many people. Yet, I felt completely alone and powerless to help.

I kept watching as the images were replayed over and over. I was in Egypt, the land of my birth. I had never thought about living elsewhere, but as I watched the events that were unfolding in New York on that day something stirred inside me and for the first time I wondered if I would live in America someday.

It seemed like a strange thought, an idea that came from nowhere. It certainly had never entered my mind before. It was something my father would not approve of. Family is everything in Egypt and to move away from your family was unthinkable.

There is something intoxicating about America, though. You can be your own person. It doesn't matter who you are, where you come from, or your family's position in society. You can be and do whatever you have the desire to. The idea that through your own hard work, sweat, and tears that you can build something with your own two hands, make a life for yourself, is wonderful and quite unique.

In Egypt success depends on other factors. The family you come from is important and while I came from a good family the opportunities that I was afforded or kept from were because of my name and had nothing to do with who I was as a person.

Of course, as much as the events of 9/11 impacted me and planted the idea of moving to America in my heart, they also caused some difficulties in making that dream a reality.

There was a lot of fear and hatred being directed at Muslims in the aftermath. I understood how it happened, but I felt burdened to explain to people that it was not all Muslims who did this terrible thing. The majority of us were peace-loving and condoned violence of that sort. In my efforts to educate others I spent time in an online chat room just talking to people, speaking out against violence and explaining that not all Muslims were alike. I had many long conversations with one young lady in particular who was an American and who was anti-Muslim. Over time attraction grew between us, we became friends, and we progressed to phone conversations.

In the months that followed 9/11 there were rumors and news reports that Muslims were being attacked and murdered in the streets in America which filled many in Egypt with great fear, including my family. Egyptians are almost by default very well liked among the different Arab cultures. That's because we're the fun ones. We like to have a good time, joke around, and just in general bring happiness to ourselves and those around us.

My mother nicknamed me "Mood" when I was younger because I could always put her in a better mood. The nickname stuck and to this day many people call me that for my ability to bring a smile to anyone's face no matter the circumstances. Today I joke that not all of my clients can understand my accent over the phone. They think I'm a telemarketer calling from India or something. So, I have learned that I can make my point and bring them a laugh by yelling into the phone, "It's Mood, I have your money!" Amazingly it doesn't matter what your accent or how thick it is, everyone can hear the word "money" perfectly fine.

I have always enjoyed making people happy, and for friends and clients I always go the extra mile. It's part of the exceptional service that I try to provide to everyone I come into contact with. I even did an Egyptian dance (with music) in the middle of Disney Springs at Walt Disney World just to make my cowriter on this book smile. Truth be told, I think that's the reason she agreed to write it with me. She just wanted to see me make an idiot of myself in public. That's fine, I'm used to jumping first and then asking "what did I get myself into" later.

Given how much I enjoy making people happy, it was deeply distressing to me that there was so much fear and hatred in the world, particularly after the terrible events of 9/11. It honestly felt like the entire world had changed in some profound way. I know it did for America. Even though what was happening was an ocean away I still felt it deeply. It was like that initial thought I had that someday I would be in America just wouldn't let go.

~

Education is extremely important in Egypt. In my family it was no exception. My parents were both incredibly hardworking, and my mother has a Ph.D. and is the dean of a college. Great importance is placed on higher education and my wife likes to tell the story about how my father always called her "Doctor" in hope and anticipation that she would go that far in her studies, his way of encouraging her.

I went to school at Mansoura University in Egypt where I studied accounting. I might not have had much money, but I did have big dreams. When I graduated I made a decision to get my CPA license. The only country in which you could get licensed was America, so people would go there from all over the world to take the exam. There were thirty of us from my class that wanted to go take it, but only six of us received visas to be able to do so. I was one of the lucky few. My plan was to go to California, take the exam, and come home. Get in, get out, don't get killed. That was the mantra.

I know that it will sound ridiculous to some people, but honestly, that's what the news reports in Egypt were leading us to believe about how things were in America. We thought there was wholesale slaughter of Muslims in the streets. Truly, it sounded as though I would be stepping into some sort of war zone and that the likelihood that I would be murdered upon arrival was fairly high. I hoped and prayed that people would take a minute to get to know me for who I was before just deciding to beat me up or kill me, but I realized that might be asking a lot.

I later discovered that, in reality, there were attacks, horrible, despicable attacks which did happen. Fortunately, though, the streets of America were not all rivers of blood as those of us in the Arab world heard and feared.

I was not the only one with concerns. My father actually had dog tags made for me for the trip to wear around my neck at all times. They stated my name and my date of birth on the front. On the back there wa a very sincere request asking that if my body was found that it be returned to the Egyptian embassy. If I was murdered in America he wanted to make sure that he knew what had happened to me and that he'd be able to at least bury me. I am not joking.

So, with a mixture of excitement and fear, very little money in my wallet, and dog tags around my neck, I boarded the plane and headed to Los Angeles.

A welcome sight

2
Coming to America

The plane finally landed in Los Angeles. We had finally made it to America and we were all terrified because we didn't know what to expect. We got off the plane and went through customs where there were police with dogs looking at everyone suspiciously. What can you do in that situation? I knew better than to crack jokes. Men with guns usually don't take those very well, especially when they're on the hunt for terrorists and smugglers.

I could feel the weight of the dog tags I was wearing, a very potent, ever-present reminder not to get myself killed. I was an only son, after all. There would be no one left to carry on the family name and I didn't need to do that to my family.

Not to mention the fact that I was pretty attached to life and I had big dreams that didn't include being gunned down in the middle of LAX for saying the wrong thing or looking at the wrong person. My mother didn't raise me to be that stupid. I figured if I just kept my head down, was quiet and polite, that was my best chance at getting out of there in one piece and not having to get shipped back to my parents in a box.

American Discovery: It doesn't matter who you are.

In the line for customs there were different groups of people, including a group of Christians from Egypt. All of them were busy laughing and joking around, not seeming to try and keep a low profile. Apparently, their mothers didn't care if they were stupid. They might have been Christians, but they were still Arabs, after all.

Meanwhile, those of us who were Muslim were nervous and quiet. We all kept our heads down, not wanting to draw attention to ourselves. In hindsight that might have actually been the best way to draw attention to ourselves, by avoiding eye contact and interaction. Way to look guilty of something! But we weren't thinking about that. We were just so worried about being hassled that was all we could do. It turned out, though, that the loud and obnoxious actions of the other group nearby ended up gaining them the attention of the wrong man.

Finally, a customs agent asked the one group why they were so boisterous while we were so quiet. They explained that we were Muslims and were worried and that they, as Christians, were not at all concerned because coming to America was like coming home for them. The customs agent sought clarification and asked if it was true that they had no concerns about making it through customs since they were Christian. They confirmed that. This group then was pulled aside and we later found out that they spent four hours in a room undergoing extensive questioning. Once they were finally allowed in their visas were only going to be valid for a few days.

That turn of events startled all of us. It taught me, though, that I couldn't make assumptions and that it didn't matter who you were or claimed you were. It didn't matter to those customs agents what religion you were. Maybe it was that other group's brazen attitudes or lack of respect that caused them trouble. I don't know to this day why they were signaled out for extra screening. I was just intensely grateful that I was not in their position.

The rest of us were still nervous going through customs, but they sent us through. A little while later when we finally made it out of the airport and I saw the big LAX sign outside I felt like I wanted to kiss the ground. I had made it into America, the land of opportunity, and for just a moment it didn't matter that I was wearing dog tags with instructions on what to do with my body.

American Discovery: The world's greatest hamburger.

We went straight to our hotel where we would be staying for two weeks. The best thing about the hotel turned out to be its location. You see, right next door was a Carl's Jr. and there I discovered the most wonderful thing. At that time they had a burger called the Six Dollar Burger. It was one of the most delicious things I'd ever eaten, and I ate it every day of those two weeks.

I was familiar with fast food. I love McDonald's French fries. In my opinion those fries are tied with air-conditioning for the most important U.S. invention. They are like getting a warm hug from your mother, a sort of homecoming. In that way it's the ultimate comfort food. In college when none of my friends or I had any money ten of us guys would all chip in to buy a large fry and we would share it. Years later when my wife was pregnant with our daughter I brought her those fries every night and she would forgive me for anything.

That Carl's Jr. burger was the best burger I'd ever had. To this day every time I drive by a Carl's Jr. or Hardee's I go in and ask them to make me one of those. It's no longer a menu item, but they still make it and I still devour them. It's a reminder of the very first thing that I came to love here in America.

The hotel served as our base of operations while we studied for the C.P.A. exams. We were also able to explore a little bit as well. The exams I had to take were held at the Anaheim Convention Center and there were a lot of people taking them all at the same time from all over the world. It was a series of four exams administered over two days. It was grueling and nerve wracking to a certain extent. We were all anxious about the outcome, but we would have to wait four weeks to know if we'd passed or not. We were all scheduled to go home well before that. At least, that was the plan.

American Discovery: This truly was a land of opportunity.

As my two weeks in America were coming to an end I was doing some research and I discovered how much CPAs in this country made. It was an astounding amount compared to what I could make back in Egypt. I realized that if I could find a job for a little while that I could send money home to help support my family. My father hadn't taken a single vacation in over twenty years and I wanted to help ease the financial burden off of him. I wanted to help pay for my sisters' weddings. I figured this was a great way to do it, and after I'd earned some money I could return home. At that moment it seemed like the simplest thing in the world. To my mind, it was as good as done.

With this plan in mind I decided to go to Florida where the woman I'd been conversing with was. I was feeling good. After all, in two whole weeks not a single person had tried to kill me and I was daydreaming about how much I could help my family with the money I was going to earn. I was feeling confident and excited when I went to the train depot to purchase a cross-country train ticket. It was here that I ran into the first of many obstacles on my road to success. What should have been a simple transaction ended up being my inaugural experience with discrimination in America.

The ticket seller wouldn't sell me a ticket for the train. He said there were no seats available. The other passengers around me started grumbling and said that he was lying, that there were seats available. A couple of them spoke up on my behald, and asked him to sell me a ticket. Even in the face of discrimination there were those who were outraged by it and kind to me which left an impression. The ticket seller steadfastly refused and said there was no way he was going to allow me onto a train. When it became clear that he was not going to budge and that there was no one else to speak to, I asked what I needed to do. Fortunately, some of the other travelers advised me to take the bus and directed me to where I needed to go.

I tried to take it in stride, figuring it would be a just fine. After all, in Egypt taking a bus is a pleasant experience. The buses there are clean, nice, have facilities, and also provide coffee and snacks on board. Taking the bus was always a relaxing experience where your needs were taken care of.

Imagine my surprise when I learned that the buses in America were not like that and the clientele on board mine was not middle or upper class but was instead a cross-section of some of the worst parts of society. It was a shock, to say the least. I wasn't permitted to take the train, though, so the bus it would have to be. Let me tell you, I had never met such an interesting and frightening group of people in my entire life.

American Discovery: Some people care about the color of your skin.

On the bus there was a young man who was very upfront about the fact that he hated and wanted to kill all white people. Apparently, I was included in that group in his mind. This was extraordinary to me because in Egypt no one cares about skin color. In fact, no one is ever described as "black" or "white". References to skin color are just not made. This was not the last time that I would encounter this kind of discrimination and this defining people by their skin color. I hated it then and I hate it now. I don't like to hear people described by their skin color. It doesn't make sense to me.

Another gentleman on the bus was a rather frightening looking guy. When I asked him what he did for a living he responded with the words, "Anything illegal". Apparently if it had to do with guns, drugs, prostitutes, or any other type of illegal activity, he was the go to guy. I found this also very disturbing as well as his absolute candor about it as I made a mental note not to antagonize him either.

Speaking of prostitutes, we had one of those on the bus as well. I believe she propositioned every man on that bus at one point or another. It was unbelievable and very uncomfortable.

Another woman on the bus turned out to have a tragic story. She was covered in bruises and we found out that she was running away from her abusive husband. She was terrified and desperately hoping that he wouldn't find her.

These were just a few of the interesting characters I shared that long bus ride with. Off we went, traveling across country from California to Florida. I did my best to avoid the young man who threatened to kill me and the young man who no doubt could sell him a weapon for the job.

The hours passed and we finally arrived at a stop in Texas where we would be boarding a new bus in a couple of hours. There was a restaurant there near the bus station that we could eat at. As we were getting off the bus the driver stopped me and then took a minute and warned me to be careful and to stay close to the station. When I asked why she pointed up at the billboard towering above us.

I quickly got the point. The billboard was promoting the military action overseas and was definitely not friendly toward Muslims.

American Discovery: You can choose your "family".

My fellow passengers took notice and an interesting thing happened. They all began to huddle around me. They reassured our bus driver that I would be just fine because they were going to take care of me and make sure no one tried to hurt me. I was amazed and beyond grateful. Even the young man who wanted me dead because of my skin color seemed determined that no one else would do me in on his watch.

They all stayed close by me for the most part and when we started to get hungry the dealer of drugs, weapons, and anything illegal took me to the restaurant. He told me to stay right with him and not talk to anyone and that he would make sure it was okay.

It was one of my first lessons about community and, indeed, family in America. People here take care of those around them. They offer help and protection. Once you have been accepted into their group they treat you like family. This idea that your "family" could be made up of people that had no blood relation to you was astonishing. It's something that I've learned to embrace in my new home.

It's amazing how many people in America call me "cousin" or "son" or something else who have no biological or marital ties to me. And they mean it when they call me part of their family. That sense of choosing your family is beautiful, and I'm constantly in awe of the lengths people go to in order to help each other out.

That bus trip took nearly four days and I saw a great deal of the country as we drove across it. I was amazed at the beauty I saw. I also was grateful for the opportunity to meet so many different people from so many different backgrounds. Most of all I was struck with the certain knowledge that this was the country I wanted to work in because I knew that it would pay me back for my hard work. I felt like if I invested my time and labor in this place it wouldn't be for nothing. Even on that bus ride with many disreputable people I felt that sense of energy, of boundless possibilities, that is at the heart of the American dream.

I told myself, "Here is a place where you can do anything, be anything. The only limits are what you place on yourself." I believe that to this day. So, even though I had very little with me I could feel that excitement, that swelling of optimism. Things were going to be wonderful!

When I finally arrived at my destination at a bus station in a small town in central Florida it was nearly midnight. I walked outside to the parking area and looked around, expecting to see someone waiting for me. I was here. I had arrived. This was the start of my great opportunity, my grand adventure. I was tired and exhilarated in equal measure. I stood there, waiting, in the middle of the night in the middle of nowhere, by myself. It began to dawn on me that something had gone wrong. My friend was supposed to pick me up, but there was no one there to greet me. I had $31 in my pocket.

In the darkness I continued to stand there, waiting. I couldn't see anything beyond the parking lot for the bus station. I stood there alone for what seemed like forever wishing I knew where my friend was and what I was supposed to do. Uncertainty began to fill me. I was a stranger in a strange land and the one person I had expected to help me was nowhere to be found.

After a very long time an employee inside the station noticed me standing outside. He came out, asked my name, and told me that someone had called and left a message for me to take a cab. I think I felt a bit of shock. It was far from the friendly welcome that I had hoped for!

I finally was able to get a taxi and he drove me to my friend's house. I had arrived at my destination and thanks to the cab fare all I had to my name was one single dollar left. Welcome to America!

Washing dishes

3
Starting at the Bottom

The next day I went out and was able to get my first job in America. I would love to say that I was using my education and training, that I was handling the books for a company or employing my accounting skills in some other way.

Alas, the only number crunching I was doing was counting the number of dishes that passed through my hands on any given day. That's right, I was washing dishes in a restaurant which is pretty the most entry level job that you can get.

Clearly it wasn't my dream job, but I had to start earning money immediately while I looked for other work. The manager wasn't deterred by hiring a man with a name he couldn't pronounce who was from Egypt and had no work experience in the country, so I got the job. For me, I was just grateful to have work anywhere at that moment. You have to do what you have to do, and I was never afraid of hard work.

While I was constantly applying and sending out resumes to other companies, I still did the job as best as I could. Every job you have gives you some kind of experience if you just bother to figure out what it is. It turns out I learned a very important lesson at that job, one of the most important, and it would serve me well for the rest of my life.

American Discovery: You can learn a lot at the bottom.

One day I saw the cook put together a plate of food, look at it for a moment, and then dump the food in the trash. I was shocked. I asked him why he did that because the food looked fine. I'll never forget his answer.

He looked me in the eyes and said, "If I wouldn't eat it, I won't serve it."

Apparently, this particular plate of food he viewed as somehow inferior, or not his best work. In his mind it wasn't fit for him and therefore it wasn't fit for the customer. I still didn't know what was wrong with that particular plate of food, I'm not sure the customer would have even known what was wrong with it, but chef did and that was what was important.

This lesson has become one of the cornerstones of my approach to working with clients. I suggest for them the things I would want for myself. If it's not good enough for me, then it is not something that is good enough for the people I work for and with. This applies to everything in my life. If a client asks me for financial advice, I give him the best I have to offer. If that same client asks me to recommend a good steakhouse, I'll take him to the best one around.

Basically, this entire principle boils down to the Golden Rule. Do unto others as you'd have done unto you. I would want someone to give me the best advice, point me to the best restaurant. If I don't want second best, then my clients shouldn't have to settle for that either.

This dedication to excellence in everything I do has served me very well, including right there in the beginning at the bottom. Believe it or not, people notice when you're doing a good job versus phoning it in. That's true whether you have a corner office with a stunning view or you're up to your elbows in dishwater and dirty plates.

It was a valuable lesson. I was grateful for the lesson and the job, but I had not come to America, traveled all the way from California to Florida, to wash dishes for the rest of my life. I viewed it as a temporary necessity until I could get one of those high paying jobs and really start helping my family back home. That was the dream, and I was determined to chase it until I had achieved that goal.

At one point I worked at a gas station and for a while I even thought that I'd own one of those someday, since the owner seemed to be doing well for himself and he was providing something that his customers very much needed. Although I never did buy a gas station, I have learned along the way to appreciate everything I do have whether it's material or not.

American Discovery: Even those at the bottom deserve respect.

While borrowing my friend's beat up old car to drive to the store one day I was pulled over by a police officer. I had seen enough American movies to know that when the police car flashed its lights you were supposed to pull over to the side. I dutifully did as I'd seen them do in the movies, all the time wondering what I'd done wrong. Once I had pulled over and parked, I started to get out of the car. The officer ordered me to stay in my vehicle. I waited anxiously, not sure how this was going to go.

I was in an old car and was not looking my best. The officer came up to my window and addressed me as "sir". I gawked at him in surprise and then just started smiling. Finally, he asked why I was smiling, and I told him it was because he had called me "sir". He might have thought I was a little crazy, but he started smiling, too.

I hadn't not expected the level of respect that he gave me just by using that one simple word. It was an eye-opener for me and really drove home that America was a nation of individuals who should be accorded respect regardless of what they were wearing, what they were driving, or how they looked. I have to tell you, the experience really had a deep impact on me and was something else I incorporated into the way I treated others.

It turned out the car had a problem and was burning oil. He pulled me over just to make sure I knew. He treated me with respect and I realized that rich or poor we were all equal in the eyes of the law. It was a great feeling.

I had dignity and self-determination, but I was still broke. I had been applying to other jobs, but was still stuck working insane hours at whatever job I could find in an attempt to make ends meet. It wasn't going so well. Given that one of the points of me staying in the country for a while was to make enough money to help support my family this was especially frustrating and it started to chip away at my confidence that this was something I could do..

I kept applying to every job I could. I found out that I had passed two of the four sections for my CPA exam and that meant that I needed to retake the other two. Unfortunately, I didn't have the time or the money to take it again. It really felt like everything I had worked for was slipping through my fingers.

To make matters worse the neighborhood I was living in was quite bad. In fact, when those I worked for found out where I was living they were very upset. I lived in a part of town that was isolated and was home to mostly criminals, particularly those with drug labs. I told those who expressed their concern that I didn't have much of a choice because it was the only place I'd been able to find where I could afford the rent.

I took to sleeping in my living room facing the front door, just in case someone tried to break in. There was absolutely nothing I had worth stealing, even for the most desperate people. Those who are under the influence of drugs and alcohol aren't known for clear thinking, though. Drugs and alcohol can make people do stupid, crazy things, like break into the poorest house in the neighborhood thinking there's something to steal. I've actually known people who died of alcohol poisoning. It's a scary, terrible thing and I've never understand how people can do that to themselves.

So, I barely slept, startling awake each night a dozen times while dozing when I'd hear an unfamiliar sound. It was a terrible way to live. Between the lack of sleep, the constant anxiety, and the brutal hours I had to put in just to afford food, things were about as bleak as they could be.

Everything that could go wrong on the path to achieving my American dream had. I had no career, no viable job prospects, a terrible relationship, no ability to move out of the place where poverty, squalor and crime were rampant, and no path to improving any of it. As things got worse and worse both at work and at home I realized that it was probably time to throw in the towel.

I had come to America with a dream and I figured it was finally time to give it up. I wasn't happy about it, but with a heavy heart I decided to chalk my American experiment up as a failure and cut my losses while I could. I didn't know what I could do differently, but I knew things couldn't stay as they were and that something had to change.

I settled on the only course of action that seemed to make sense to me at that point. I decided to go back to Egypt.

American Discovery: Kids come first.

This isn't necessarily an idea that's unique to America, but it is a lesson I learned while in America. In fact, had I not learned it when I did, it's very possible I'd be living in Egypt today.

After six months of living in Florida I was ready to give up on everything – the dream, my career, even the woman I was married to at the time. At that point there had been too many disappointments and frustrations that I felt were insurmountable and I felt that staying would just be futile.

So, I packed up my few things, bought a one-way ticket back to Egypt and headed for the airport. I kid you not that I was halfway to the airport when I got a call that changed my entire life. It was my soon-to-be ex-wife calling. She revealed to me that she had just discovered that she was pregnant. I was in shock at the news, but I quickly turned the car around and headed back home.

A few months later my son, Mohamed, was born. Everything in my life became about taking care of and providing for him. I worked eighteen hours a day to feed my family. No matter what I did I couldn't seem to get ahead. I started working multiple jobs and I was barely sleeping. Even when I did sleep there was a looming fear that kept me half awake much of the time.

I still believed deep down that there had to be a better way, that somewhere there was an opportunity waiting for me. I was just getting mighty tired of waiting for it. I also had two families now that I felt I couldn't take care of: the one here in Florida and the one back in Egypt.

I had turned into a zombie. I was walking through my day fortified by very little sleep and very little hope. Things might have been easier at that point if it weren't for the other problems that I was encountering at the time.

I lived in what I had come to understand was a dangerous neighborhood. Even worse than that I found myself the target of discrimination from pretty much anyone you could think of. I was the only Egyptian in town and it seemed that no one was happy that I was there.

I got a job working at a convenience store. There I would have an opportunity to learn even more about customer service than I had in my previous jobs. I also ran afoul of more discrimination and prejudice than ever before, and it took an extraordinary experience to overcome it all.

My son

4
Discrimination and Death Threats

When I got the job working at the convenience store I worked Mondays through Saturdays from six in the morning until ten at night and Sundays from seven in the morning until nine at night. I worked every hour it was open, seven days a week. It was grueling work. I did the stocking and ran the cash register. We sold a lot of different things in that store including live bait for fishermen. In the front window area there were a couple of tables and chairs set up where some of the older men would come and sit all day just to be out of their houses. They'd talk to each other and to me and tell stories.

It was an interesting place and it did good business, but it reeked of the kind of despair that you find anywhere that there is abject poverty. Still, I worked as hard as I could, arranging things so that it would be the best shopping experience for the clients.

While working at the convenience store, it was brought to my attention that not everyone in the small town where I was living appreciated having to interact with a Muslim from Egypt. Several made that clear in no uncertain terms. They spray painted obscene epithets on the outside of the store where I was working. They'd come inside and tell me to my face that if they caught me on the street outside they'd kill me in a heartbeat. They made sure I saw the guns they had that they planned to use on me.

All I could do was stare at them and tell them that they could not stop me from working and they knew where to find me since I was almost always at the store. Unfortunately, I knew they also knew where I lived. I was living in a mobile home in a very rundown and dangerous area of town. I had a young son at home and was constantly worried for his safety. I was fairly certain that they were going to kill me, but I had no idea what else I could do.

I did my best to be friendly and non-combative even in the face of the hatred. I provided excellent customer service to everyone, regardless of whether they wanted to kill me or not.

American Discovery: Apparently, people have different opinions about my race.

It seemed like no matter who I was interacting with in town, people took exception with my perceived race or skin color. As I said earlier, judging someone based on the color of their skin was shocking to me. Still, it was happening here constantly. The ironic part was that there was disagreement as to which category I fell into.

I went to a barber to get a haircut and when I stepped foot inside the shop everyone inside immediately stopped talking and started staring at me. For the life of me I couldn't figure out why. I sat down in a chair that I was directed to, and the man who would be cutting my hair towered over me, glaring. He asked me what I wanted.

I told him I just needed a simple haircut, that I preferred to keep my hair quite short. He took an electric razor and in a couple of seconds shaved the center of my head so that it resembled a reverse mohawk. Then he told me to get out. I was stunned. I asked him why he had done this to me. He said that I had a lot of nerve going into that shop and never to show my white face in their again. I tried to point out that I was not, indeed, "white", but to him and all the rest of the people in there I most certainly was. I got another earful, most of it spewing hate, and I scurried out of there.

The experience really shook me up. Of course, to others in town, I was definitely not seen as "white". I will never forget the horror of finding the outside of the building where I was working spray painted with the words "sand n****r go home".

Cleaning off spray painted words of hate became almost a daily part of my work routine. People were creative. They attacked my religion, my ethnicity, my perceived color, pretty much anything you can think of. It was as though I had become the center of all racial aggression in the entire town. Maybe it's because I was the only Muslim, certainly the only Egyptian. I was to them an outsider who had no business being there.

I did my best to be polite to everyone and not to give back what I got. It was very hard sometimes, but I needed the work, and I had a family to think and worry about. I was doing my best to live by that golden rule. You know one of the funny things? I was attacked for being Muslim, but growing up we had more Bibles in our house than any of the people attacking me likely had in theirs.

My mom was the dean of a college, and she had a doctorate in medieval architecture, much of which is Christian churches. I grew up with Bibles. I had read the Bible. I could tell you how many times Jesus was mentioned in the Quran and that he is revered in Islam and his name blessed when he is mentioned. I understood the golden rule, and wished others were trying harder to apply it. I was trying, but nothing I did seemed to matter to my neighbors, my customers, or anyone else I interacted with. I knew that things could not continue indefinitely as they were, but I was at a loss as to how to fix it.

Even as things were coming to a head with the discrimination I was facing, there was still plenty of opportunity to find humor even in unexpected situations. You want to know who doesn't discriminate based on your ethnicity or culture? The U.S. government, that's who.

American Discovery: Selective service is for everyone.

In Egypt, carrying on the family line and the family name is culturally very important. For example, because I am the only son, I would not be allowed to serve in the military since if I was killed there would be no brothers who could carry on the family name. Literally, I could not serve.

So, a couple weeks after getting my Florida driver's license when I received the notification to sign up for selective services I assumed that I would be exempt. First off, I wasn't a citizen and besides, I was an only son. I dutifully called the number on the notice and had a very different conversation than the one I was expecting.

After I had explained my situation the man on the other end of the line asked me, "Do you plan on staying in this country for more than six months?" I told him that was most certainly my intention. Then he asked, "Do you plan on working and earning money in this country?" I told him of course I did. I mean, after all, that was kind of the point of my even being there in the first place.

He then told me, "If you're going to live in this country and earn money in this country then you should be willing to defend this country." I couldn't argue with him on that point, so I was signed up that day.

I was now able to be drafted if the country went to war. It was not lost on me, though, that I was more likely to die a violent death in this country than die fighting for it.

Working at the convenience store

5
The Storm

A crisis can bring out the best in people. Unfortunately, it can also bring out the worst. For every story about heroes running into burning buildings to save people there are also stories of people taking advantage of disasters to loot, burn, destroy property, and commit even worse crimes. I have noticed that disasters are very polarizing in that way.

I remember the images of the firefighters who risked their life trying to save people from the twin towers. So many heroes did what they could to help. Actors worked in kitchens feeding the first responders side-by-side with people from all other walks of life.

I would see images on television of storms or other disasters around the country and how American citizens would rally together to save lives and provide food and shelter to those who lost everything. Of course, the images of devastation and destruction that were shown were often far more potent and the death count is always horrifying when tragedy strikes. The breakdown in law and order that can occur is also a frightening thing to contemplate, particularly if you're already not on the best terms with your neighbors.

It was the summer of 2004 and by this point tensions had mounted to an unbearable level. The death threats against me had escalated and it really did just seem like a matter of time before someone tried to follow through. I had nowhere else I could go, no money with which I could move my family. I decided the smartest thing to do until things calmed down was to send my little boy to live with relatives out of state for a little while as I tried to get this situation resolved. It nearly destroyed me to do it, but I couldn't risk him getting hurt.

My decision seemed even more timely when the news broke that a hurricane was bearing down on Florida and that the expected destruction could be vast. It was my first experience with this kind of a storm. I didn't know exactly what to expect and I was nervous as everyone around me started preparing for the worst.

American Discovery: Everyone is a neighbor in a storm.

Hurricane Charley arrived in August of 2004 and devastated several parts of Florida. It was a category 4 storm with winds of 150 miles per hour when it first struck the state. In anticipation of the storm I helped the owner board up all the windows and doors for the convenience store and I went home to ride out the hurricane, fearful of what might happen. I lost power early which heightened my anxiety.

Finally, there was a pounding on my door. I figured my tormenters had come to kill me, masked as they would be by the storm. Holding a long knife behind my back I opened the front door. Sure enough, a couple of the same people who had been shoving guns in my face and threatening to kill me just a few short days before were standing there. I tightened my grip on the knife knowing I wasn't going to survive their attack.

Only the attack didn't come. They stared at me in fear and explained that there was a baby at home and they needed supplies urgently for the baby, but every place was shut up tight and they couldn't get to another town. They begged me for help, asking me to open the store and sell them what they needed.

I was so relieved. I told them I understood. I went down to the store, pried the wood off the front door, and went inside. I sold them what they needed. Word spread rapidly that I was open and as the storm raged people needed more and more supplies and other things. I stayed in that store for three full days without leaving, helping everyone who came in. When it was all over the shelves were completely bare as I had sold every single item in that convenience store.

More importantly, I had earned the trust and respect of my community. During that crisis I had an opportunity to show my character to them and they were able to see past my nationality and my religion and get to know me as a person. That storm changed everything.

The very people who had been threatening to kill me now treated me as a friend. I had seventy-six invitations to Thanksgiving dinner a few months later and since I could clearly not attend all of them people kept bringing food to my house for the next couple of days. I had more turkey than I knew what to do with. That storm helped make me a welcomed part of the community.

Proud to be an American.

It addition to helping me find acceptance in the community, the storm and its aftermath also made me really feel for the first time that I was an American. In my heart I wasn't just living here, I belonged here. I was home. This was something I could never get my father to understand. Where once I had thought of my stay in America as temporary now I felt like I was part of it.

In Egypt, families are expected to stay together, and the son eventually becomes responsible for the family as he grows to be a man. By deciding to stay in America I was not only going against tradition but I was also deeply upsetting my father. Every single day he would call me and ask me when I was moving home. Every single day I told him that I already was home, that America was my home. No matter how many times I told him that I was already home he still refused to accept it.

America had become my home, though. I put in my blood, sweat, and tears hoping and believing that I, too, would soon be living the American dream despite my circumstances. I just knew that the key was working hard and providing people with what they needed. To do that I was willing to go the extra mile.

All my efforts, particularly during the hurricane, had been paying off as far as my connection with those around me. As the people opened up to me I was able to provide them with better and better service at the store. When I saw someone pull up outside, I'd have whatever they usually came in to buy ready and waiting at the cash register for them by the time they could walk inside. In many regards I was their own personal shopping concierge.

This skill came in handy when a hurricane in a different state resulted in thousands of cases of drinks and other groceries that couldn't be delivered to the afflicted state ended up being delivered instead to our store. We were so overloaded that there was no room anywhere for anything else. I decided that this wasn't a problem, but rather an opportunity to provide even higher service.

When customers came in I told them that we were having a sale and that they should stock up and get everything for the discounted price instead of having to come back in a week or a month to buy more at full price. People that came in for one or two things ended up leaving with dozens of items. Within three days I had sold all of the excess goods that had been shipped to us. It seemed like an impossible task, but I had the can-do spirit to help me get it done.

One of the things I have always admired about my fellow American citizens is that when bad things happen they all roll up their sleeves and pitch in to fix it and get things done. That storm gave me an opportunity to do that for my community and it's something that has stayed with me. It's something that I do whenever I can, and it led me years later to one of the most profound experiences of my life.

Looking like a banker

6
Nearly Losing the American Dream

I had finally been accepted in my community which was great. They dubbed me the "Egyptian Redneck" and even got me a bumper sticker for my car saying that. They also gifted me with a belt buckle that had my name engraved on the inside. I took to listening to country music, and I really felt welcomed and like one of them. That was the great thing about those days and weeks after the hurricane, that sense of belonging and acceptance. I had worked hard to earn it and was so grateful when I got it.

The downside was that I was still working eighteen hours a day while raising an infant son who was turning into a toddler. Some days I had to work the third shift at the gas station in town after I got off work at the convenience store. Despite the long hours I still couldn't provide for my family. I was barely eating let alone sleeping. I was beyond exhausted and absolutely nothing had panned out. No matter how many jobs I applied to it didn't seem to matter. I was chasing the illusive American dream, and with each day that passed it seemed to be getting farther and farther away.

It was nearly impossible to keep my hopes alive as I struggled with the despair that comes from abject poverty and a seeming inability to better one's situation. The dilapidated house we lived in was in the worst possible neighborhood. Apparently, I was the only one in the area who wasn't either a meth dealer or an addict. I worried about the environment in which I was raising Mohamed and I struggled to remind myself what I was fighting for. Every day grew harder and harder.

By the spring of 2005 I was beyond desperate. When I couldn't pay the electric bill and the power was turned off to the house I had to listen to my son wailing in the middle of the night because of the extreme heat. For the only time in my life I seriously contemplated suicide because the pain and despair were very great. I felt that I had failed as a man and a father.

Then, a miracle happened. I got the phone call that would change my life forever. Someone had decided to take a chance on me, and they offered me a part-time position as a bank teller. I would work just a couple of hours a day with minimal pay. But I was finally going to be working in finance, the field I had studied!

My boss at the convenience store allowed me to take off the hours that I needed for the bank. So, I would open the store at six in the morning. When the owner came in at nine I would make sandwiches and fried chicken in the deli portion of the store for an hour-and-a-half. Then I'd race over to the bank, work there until three in the afternoon then return to the store and work as the cashier until closing at ten. So, my hours didn't change, I was just splitting them between the two locations. Even though my schedule was still impossibly grueling, that ember of hope returned within me.

The only problem was that I had reached the point where I literally could not stand being apart from my son. I missed him so much that I began to carry him on my shoulder while I was working. My mother's old nickname for me, Mood, was catching on here, and now my son was called Mini Mood.

Your dreams aren't just magically handed to you on a silver platter when you turn twenty-one. No, you have to work hard for them. You have to be willing to put in the effort, to go above and beyond what the next guy in line is willing to do. I had been putting in a hundred hours a week at the convenience store while I was still constantly applying for a job in finance. It wasn't easy. It wasn't fun. It took everything I had and then some to keep going. And when I finally got that first banking job I couldn't ease off for a while and congratulate myself on the achievement. No! I pushed harder, worked smarter and faster. I did everything I could to stand out because my goal was not to be a bank teller. My goal was to be the man who owned the bank. Being a teller was just the first step on that path, not the last. It wasn't even close to the middle. At least I had started, though. I was finally on the path that I wanted to be on, and I couldn't have been happier about it.

One of the tellers at the bank was especially kind to me and finally got me a nametag that had my nickname, Mood, on it so that people could at least pronounce my name. That was actually really helpful. I worked as hard as I could at that position, giving the same exceptional customer service that I had been giving at the convenience store. I began to win over my coworkers and customers there as well. My efforts did not go unnoticed by management. My name started getting noticed and finally I moved up from part-time teller to relationship banker. I was one of the guys who had a desk with a nameplate that had my full name on it.

When I was working one day a woman and her twenty-year-old son came in to open up a checking account. The son looked at the nameplate on my desk and then looked at me. He asked, "How did they ever give a guy with that name a job working here?"

I looked him straight in the eyes and said, "Because you never applied."

My answer took him by surprise and he told me he didn't understand.

I told him it was simple. Just imagine if we had both submitted an application for the same entry level job at the bank. With those two applications sitting in front of him the manager would hire the man whose name he could easily pronounce. But, fortunately, for me, this young man hadn't applied for the job, so I got it instead.

I blew his mind. Ultimately, I think he got the point I was trying to express. So many people look at what others have and wonder why they don't have it. Oftentimes the answer is that the person who got it asked and the person who didn't stayed silent. If you want something you have to go for it and try with all your might. It might take you what seems forever to get it, but you need to stay the course. You need to work to make the American dream your American reality.

From relationship banker I then was licensed to offer insurance products, and in no time I became one of the top licensed bankers in our firm. I didn't settle down at that point. Instead I buckled down and worked even harder. My clients at the grocery store became my clients at the bank. The same people who had once treated me horribly were now investing funds in my institution.

I still employed the golden rule, treating others as I wished to be treated. One day a gentleman came into the branch. His wife had just died suddenly, and she had taken care of the finances. He knew nothing. I sat with him for hours over several days, helping him get everything in order, showing him how to balance his checkbook. He had only a few hundred dollars at any given time, but I helped him get through the confusion of those days.

My coworkers always asked me why I bothered to spend so much time helping him. He had no money and he would never be investing anything with us. I told them that I helped him, because it was the right thing to do. I didn't need a reason beyond that.

A few months later the man came back in one day and came straight to me. He sat down and asked me if I handled investments. I told him that I did. He handed me a check for 1.5 million dollars and asked if I could do something with it for him. It turned out his wife had actually died as a result of medical malpractice and that this was just the first check of several that was part of the settlement.

I was happy to help him, and he made me promise I wouldn't tell his children about the money. He didn't want them knowing or treating him differently because of it. When he died a few years later his daughter called me and said that he had left instructions to call me. She was beside herself. She had no idea why he had wanted her to call me, but she confided in me that they were worried and scared because they didn't even have enough money to bury him.

I told her not to worry, I would handle everything. I made all the funeral arrangements and when it was over I was able to tell her and her one brother that their father had left them a small fortune. Being able to help this family through all of these circumstances was important to me. All my clients have always been important to me.

I want the American dream for everyone,
especially my children.

7
The American Dream

Everyone knew "Mood" and I started getting recognition in different bank functions around the country. It was brought home to me that, even if it takes time, hard work truly does pay off in the end. I went from a banker to the assistant branch manager.

One day that I will never forget a guy walked into the branch and claimed that I messed up his account (which, of course, I hadn't), and that he was going home to get his machine gun and come back to kill me. At that point it had been about two years since the last time someone threatened to kill me. This time, though, I didn't have to face it alone. Corporate security was called, and they sent me a bodyguard who sat outside my office for a week.

In early 2007 I had the opportunity to open my own branch. I went and hired the most diversified team that my bank had ever seen. My team members came from the Caribbean islands, India, Columbia, Egypt, and Midwest America. They nicknamed our branch the International Branch. It was a beautiful small team that represented the melting pot America was built on. Our diversity was its strength and our American Dream was our bond.

My branch was always a top performer. When other managers asked me how my branch was always number one, I would tell them, "I buy my team friend chicken and okra for breakfast from Walmart almost every day."

The bank had 2,000 branches and I was quickly named the top Branch Manager. While other managers worked 40 hours I worked 80 hours, and right then I quit working at grocery stores or gas stations even on the weekends.

I had decided to raise Mohamed by myself, and I was able to buy a house for the two of us. That was the day that I felt like I had actually achieved the American dream, because I now owned a small piece of America. That house and the land it stood on were mine. It was truly overwhelming.

It was amazing how much things had changed in just two years. I felt like it was an affirmation of that feeling I had on that cross-country bus trip in 2003. I had believed then that this was a place where if you worked hard, the investment in time and energy would pay off.

American Discovery: Sometimes you have to take a risk.

2008 arrived and with it the housing crisis and financial collapse. I saw banks failing rapidly. I had been making good money and had just bought the house. However, I needed more flexible hours to take care of my son. I also needed to increase my income so I could help back home with my family, especially since my sisters were getting ready to get married.

I'm the kind of guy who doesn't like comfort zones. I also believe there is no progress in standing still. It's like the difference between a swamp and a waterfall. One is stagnant and the other is constantly moving. Which one do you like more?

While everyone was running away from Wall Street, I decided to become a financial advisor and bring Wall Street to Main Street. Everyone told me I was crazy. I had bought a house, took on responsibility to raise my son alone, and left a big salary for a mainly fee based business.

I kid you not, I lost a lot of hair that year. I had to take the Series 7 (General Securities Representative) and Series 66 (NASAA Uniform Combined State Law) exams. Most people take three months to study for and take the exams. Only about a third pass it on their first attempt. I didn't have three months. I had ten days.

I brought my mother from Egypt to help me with Mini Mood while I was studying . This was my introduction to coffee which enabled me to stay up for the 48 hours leading up to the exam. I passed and started a new chapter in my life.

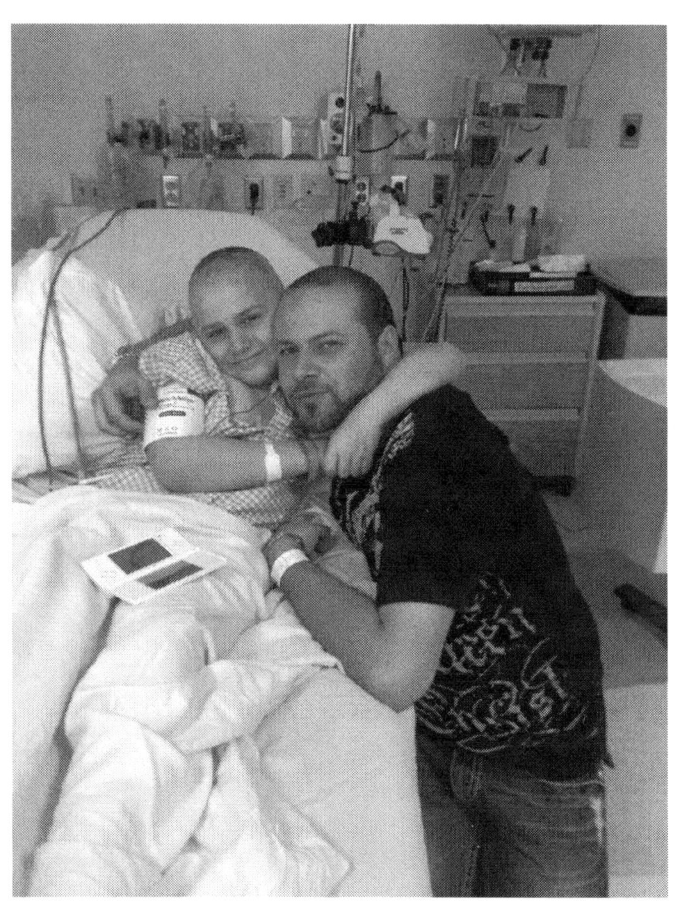

In the hospital with my son

8
Everything Changes

Now what? Just a few days after I got my licenses and I was ready to roll guess what happened? Lehman Brothers went down followed by hundreds of financial institutions going bankrupt. The financial news tape was red and hundreds of thousands of people were losing their jobs. Everyone was losing money. Everyone was scared of even saying the word "market", and here I was, the new kid on the block, asking them to believe in me and invest their entire life savings with me.

I'll never forget the day my mom left and went back to Egypt and it was just Mohamed and me. I didn't know what to do and how to take on the responsibility by myself. I was going to have to be both father and mother to him. So, Mohamed and I decided that we would be a team. Every morning before dropping him off for school we would say together, "Me and you against the world".

It was a bootcamp lifestyle for Big Mood and Mini Mood. We would open our eyes at six a.m., shower, get dressed, pray morning prayers, make breakfast, get in the car and listen to The Quran, drop him at daycare, then head to the crazy world of 2008.

Going to the office was a bad idea because morale was down and all the news was very negative. So, I decided to try to meet as many prospects as possible and my car truly became my office in the hours between 7 a.m. and 6 p.m. each day. By the end of 2008 I had driven nearly 120,000 miles.

Picking up Mohamed from daycare was the major event that I waited for every day. I couldn't wait for my little buddy to tell me how his day was and what he learned. We would drive home, and on the way he would give me the menu for dinner. Yes, I learned how to cook just for him. Before I didn't even know how to make a cup of tea, but thanks to the telephone my mom taught me how to cook. In no time I became really good at it.

My son never cared for fast food. He always wanted to eat home-cooked food and loved to stay home. God knew what I already had on my plate, so he blessed me with a very easy child to handle.

Mohamed would sit at the kitchen counter doing his homework while I was cooking. Then we would sit and eat. After that he cleaned the table and helped with the dishes. We would then watch some cartoons, play some Wii, and then he would be in bed at 8:30 sharp. I would start to read to him and he'd be asleep in seconds. I then had a couple of hours to study for my M.B.A. or catch up on work.

Mohamed started watching market news with me. After all he really had no choice since this was what I was watching all day long and at the age of 4 he knew the different market indices along with different portfolio options. So, whenever the market was down big he would tell me, “Dad, you need to call your clients”. When the market was green he would say, “Dad, you need to get more clients”.

He was my junior partner in every way. We can’t remember how many times he did his homework in the car when I was driving to meetings or how many times he fall asleep on my shoulder while I was doing client reviews at their home at night.

~

My name really started getting out there. My clients were referring all their friends and family members to me. I became a Vice President. I was really on a roll, and I was excited by all the opportunities that seemed to be opening up for me. Even more than that I was excited that I was able to provide more and more services for my clients. As my financial aspirations were finally coming to fruition another miracle walked into my life quite literally.

I will never forget the first time that I saw Marim. I was at a bookstore when she walked in with a friend. I saw her come through the door and I knew right then and there that I wanted to marry this woman. She was beautiful, smart, and something deep inside told me this was the woman of my dreams. I talked to her and found out just how funny she was and kind. She was everything. I was thrilled to discover that the attraction was mutual.

However, one thing stood in our way. Her father wouldn't give us permission to marry. She was still in college and I was ten years older than her and had a young son. In his eyes this was not a good match for his daughter. I did everything I could to change his mind. I asked, I begged, I tried time and time again to win his approval and convince him to let us be together. As many times as I could ask he would be quick with saying no.

It was agony. I had a great job, a wonderful son, but without Marim I felt like our lives weren't complete. Still, life was so much better than it ever had been, and I was filled with love and optimism. We had come so far, and I felt that her father's repeated refusal to give his blessing was just another obstacle to overcome.

Mohamed and I went to Egypt to visit my sister who was having a baby. Everything was wonderful, exciting, and things just kept getting better every day.

That's when life took a sudden dark turn that made the twenty-hour days steeped in poverty feel like they had not been as bad as I remembered.

~

While we were in Egypt I noticed that Mohamed was becoming very pale. He completely lost his appetite and started having unexplained pain. Black bruises began to appear on his body. I asked him if he was playing rough or running into things and he told me he had no energy for playing rough and had no idea where the bruises were coming from.

As soon as we got back to the states I took him to his pediatrician who ran some tests and immediately asked me to get some blood work done on him. We did so right away, and then went home. I'll never forget that moment when my phone rang while he and I were on the coach watching television. When I saw his doctor's name on the phone I realized it was something bad because doctors never call you at night.

I answered, and the doctor told me that I needed to take Mohamed to the hospital right away. I knew it was really bad when she recommended that we pack a bag and take it with us. We did just that and hurried to the hospital. In the car on the way there Mohamed asked me, "Dad, am I going to die?"

I don't know why he asked, but I answered him back very firmly, "Not before me."

We got to the hospital and they immediately took us into the ER and started running every test you can imagine. They moved us up to a room, and the doctor come to me saying that it might be a very bad infection and that they would need to keep Mohamed for a few days.

The next day the doctors came and said they found out it was Leukemia, but that he believed it was probably ALL which was 92% curable. He said treatment was easy, but they would need to take some bone marrow to make sure that's what it was.

They took the bone marrow. When the test results came in they called me outside Mohamed's room. The doctor, a nurse, and a social worker were all standing there looking at me in a weird way. The doctor asked me if I had any other kids. When I told him I didn't, they all looked down.

I knew something was terribly wrong. Finally, the doctor told me that it was actually AML, a very aggressive kind of leukemia. He told me that only 500 kids in the world get that type each year. He then went on to tell me that the cancer was in 75% of Mohamed's body. Finally, he delivered the worst news. He told me that my son had only six weeks to live.

I don't know what they expected me to say or how they expected me to respond. Obviously the news was horrific. I looked the doctor in the eyes and I told him to do his job, and that all those numbers meant nothing to me. I told him that God gave me Mohamed for a reason and that God would save him for an even bigger reason.

I don't know which was worse—hearing the news or knowing that I had to go back to my son's room and tell him the news.

I wanted to scream so bad, but I couldn't because Mohamed would hear me. I wanted to cry, but I couldn't because I knew I needed to stay strong for him. Blood vessels started to blow up in my eyes from the stress, but finally I went to the room and told him the news.

I don't know where he got that strength or faith from, but he very calmly said, "Thank God". We would always thank God for everything and he was going to continue doing so.

The amazing thing is that Mohamed and I had actually been volunteering in a non-profit helping kids with cancer before all this took place, so he kind of knew what to expect. Since we had been around these kids and had a chance to talk to him we were familiar with the trials that he'd be facing. He knew about losing hair, the pain from the chemo, the headaches, the bone marrow surgeries, and much more of what those fighter angels go through. What neither of us knew, was everything that would happen next.

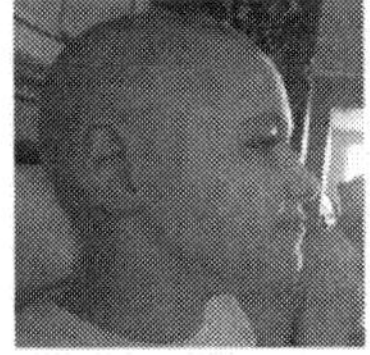

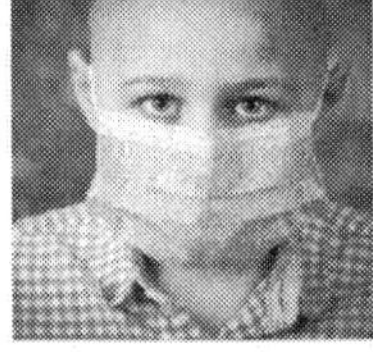

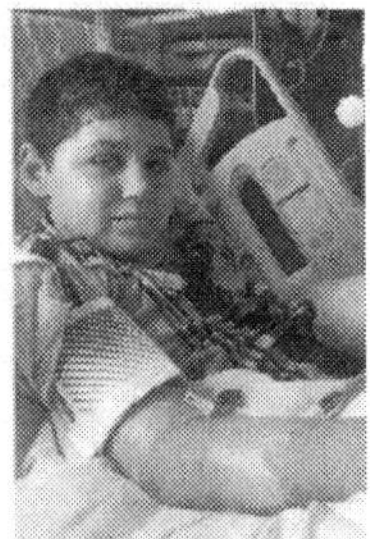

Some people never meet their HERO

I gave birth to mine

Support Childhood Cancer Awareness

9
Love and Prayer Know No Boundaries

Until you've been there you can't understand the horror of hearing that your child has a terminal illness. Mohamed was admitted to the hospital immediately and they began doing treatments on him. My sweet, brave boy was cheerful and upbeat the entire time. Every day he'd say, "I thank Allah that I'm still alive."

Cancer doesn't discriminate. It can attack anyone regardless of faith, race, gender, or even age. The thought that my young son was going to have to face such a brutal, ruthless enemy was heart breaking. Both he and I refused to give up.

Miraculous things began to happen almost instantaneously. The first week that he was in the hospital all my friends and clients told everyone they knew that he needed prayer. He had 431 visitors in that first week, all there to gather around his bed and pray for him. Christians from various churches, Muslims from different mosques, and Jews from one of the synagogues all gathered side-by-side around Mohamed to pray over him. I was amazed and overwhelmed by the outpouring of love. The majority of these people didn't know him or me, but they responded to a call for prayer for this sick young boy.

Even the hospital staff was amazed at the love and support that so many were showing for my son. Through it all he remained sweet and upbeat and full of faith. He became an inspiration to many.

At one point they had taken so much blood from him that it reached the point where they couldn't get more to come out. So, they reached out to the helicopter crew because they are highly trained to take blood in any situation. They came to his room which was full of doctors and tried to get blood from the IV in his arm, but it still wouldn't work. Finally they tried taking the blood from his foot when he firmly said, "Stop". He then told them to try the IV again when he said to start. Everyone got quiet and he began reading the Quran out loud. The blood started flowing, and the nurses told him to keep on reading and not to stop whatever he was saying.

Marim, the woman I was in love with, and her father came to visit Mohamed in the hospital. They made it before my family who was flying in from Egypt a couple of days later. Something about that experience softened her father's heart. Then again, seeing a young boy fighting such a deadly disease gave everyone who saw him a chance to pause and reflect on the uncertainty and the preciousness of life and it changed many lives.

Her father pulled me aside and what he said next surprised me. He told me that it was clear that I loved Marim and that she loved me. He said it was useless at this point to try and keep us apart, and that I could marry her. His one condition was that he wanted us married within the week.

It had to be one of the most insanely fast weddings of that magnitude that has ever been put together. A client of mine who was a wedding planner handled everything. Another client who was a DJ provided the music. The restaurant that I always ate lunch in volunteered to cater when they found out what was happening. My parents made it to Florida just in time for the wedding. It was so crazy. I was living my dream and my nightmare all at the same time.

Months went by and Mohamed kept fighting for life. Hundreds of people donated blood on his behalf. Something for which we were wildly grateful. To this day our family donates blood when we can in gratitude for those who did so for us in our time of greatest need.

The six weeks the doctors had given him to live passed, and he was still alive, still fighting. He was still cheerful and grateful for every day. People of all faiths continued to come together to pray for him. I thought I had a gift for winning people over through perseverance and good will. It turns out Mohamed has a gift for bringing people to together just by his very nature.

Months passed and to the shock of the doctors Mohamed began to get better. They claimed that it was a miracle because there was no explanation for what they were seeing. Mohamed asked me if he could have two things once he recovered. I would have given him anything he asked at that point. His first request was for a puppy. He was a very typical child in that way. Yes, he got the puppy. The second request he had was going to be much more difficult to pull off. He wanted to visit the three most holy sites.

The three holy sites in Islam are: Masjid al Haram in Mecca, Masjid al Nabawi in Medina, and Al-Aqsa, in Jerusalem. The first two are in Saudi Arabia and were going to be much easier for us to get to than the third. I just did not know how I was going to pull this off. But, I made a promise to my son. When he beat the leukemia we would go.

American Discovery: You never know who might be able to help you out.

The miracles surrounding Mohamed and his recovery kept coming. His desire to go on this trip was no exception. About the time it looked like he might be able to leave the hospital I received an email from a travel company based out of New York letting me know that for the first time a tour to all three mosques was available.

I could hardly believe my eyes, particularly since I had never heard of this company and didn't work with them in any way. I called the number and the lady informed me that they did indeed have two spots available. She said she had no idea how I had come to be on their mailing list either. Excitement started to build in me at the prospect of fulfilling my son's second request. Then I hit a problem.

I told her that we needed to go to Egypt first in order to visit family. She told me that was quite impossible since everyone taking the tour had to leave together from New York. She insisted that there was no way for Mohamed and me to join up with the tour in Saudi Arabia. I was angry and disappointed by the time I hung up.

I turned around and noticed a gentleman coming out of the hospital. He was a friend of a man I met one day in the hospital elevator. I had been briefly introduced. He was an acquaintance of an acquaintance, but he recognized me and asked me what was wrong.

I explained to him what had happened and he asked me which travel company I had been speaking with. I told him. He asked me if I would wait for five minutes while he made a quick phone call. I agreed and he walked out of my earshot. A minute later he began walking back toward me when my phone rang.

It was the lady I had been speaking to at the tour company. She asked me if I knew who the man standing with me was. I confessed that I didn't. She then informed me that this passing acquaintance was, in fact, the owner of that travel company. She said that he had worked everything out and that there would be no problem with us going to Egypt first.

The doctor cleared Mohamed for travel, and we were soon on our way. After spending time in Egypt with family we were able to join the tour group. On that very special trip I saw even more of my son's ability to bring people together.

At Mecca

At Medina

At Jerusalem

10
Moving Mountains

Mohamed finally got out of the hospital in December. Thanks to all the time Marim had spent with him in the hospital studying, he was actually skipped ahead in school when he was able to return. That was an unexpected blessing.

When spring break rolled around it was time for our much anticipated trip to visit the three mosques. My wife, Marim, was pregnant with our daughter and would remain at home fearing for us and saying many prayers for our safety. I will say this, being American citizens helped us greatly on the journey at several different points. Throughout our journey we also felt incredibly blessed.

When we went to Masjid al Haram in Mecca it was an amazing experience for so many reasons. Safa and Marwa are two hills that are a part of the place. They rest about 1,500 feet apart from each other. When Abraham's wife Hagar and her son Ishmael were starving in the desert without food and water, Hagar passed back and forth between the two hills seven times in search of water. An angel finally caused a well to spring up next to Ishmael, saving mother and child.

It is tradition to jog back and forth between the two hills seven times as Hagar did.

At that time Mohamed was still working to regain the muscle that had atrophied during his long hospital stay and he started out the journey limping. Without saying a word two men jogged picked him up under the arms and carried him to the hill. They set him down and two other men picked him up and jogged him back. This went on with two different men carrying him each time until he had completed the seven trips. When it was finished all of these people formed a circle around Mohamed and brought water from the well and poured it over him. It was the most miraculous, moving experience. They didn't know us, but they felt compelled to bless him in that way.

When we made our way to pray, even though hundreds of thousands were crowded in to do the same thing, people moved, making a path so that Mohamed could get right at the front where they somehow made room for us. As he passed by, strangers kept rising and kissing him on the head. I had never seen anything like this in my life.

When we visited Masjid al Nabawi in Medina people again made room for Mohamed and treated him with great respect. Again we had a powerful spiritual experience.

After this we finally came to what was going to be the most difficult part of our journey, the border crossing before we could get to Jerusalem. All of us on the tour bus were U.S. citizens, but we were also Muslim and most of us were born in other countries.

Israeli soldiers boarded the bus with automatic weapons and instructed us all to hold our passports over our heads.

There was a nervous ripple throughout the bus. It was compounded moments later when my son started excitedly pointing out what types of guns the soldiers were carrying. Thanks to a nurse who had taught him how to play Call of Duty at nights in the hospital he knew what all the weapons were and was excited to see them in real life and share his knowledge about their capabilities. I kept telling him to be quiet as I could feel others around me beginning to panic more. The soldiers were smiling, but their fingers never left the triggers of their weapons the entire time.

One older gentleman was born in Pakistan. When one of the soldiers asked him what he did for a living he responded that he was retired. When asked what he'd done before he retired he told them he was a biochemical engineer. At that point the whole busload of us was sure that we'd had it. The soldier started laughing and asked, "Did you honestly just say that?"

The older man said, "Yes."

The soldier said, "You know we're going to have to detain you for further questions."

With a smile the man said, "But, son, I'm retired."

With an equally broad grin the soldier answered, "But, dad, it doesn't matter."

The two of them were busy laughing over it while the rest of us were sweating bullets. In the end they did detain him for questioning along with more than two-thirds of the rest of the tour group. Much to my relief,

Mohamed and I were two of the very few who were admitted without further questioning. Unfortunately, the tour group leaders were all detained. As they were walking away with the soldiers they yelled at me, "Mahmoud! Take care of the others."

No pressure, right? I had never been to Jerusalem before, but when the bus driver got us to the hotel I was able to handle the check-in and get everyone into their rooms. I spoke Arabic and no one else in our group did. The Israelis we dealt with spoke no English, but they did speak Arabic so I was the only one who could communicate with them. Two of the families that had been let through were very upset because for each of them their twenty-year-old daughters had been detained. I reached out to the embassy that was close to our hotel, and we finally got the daughters released.

After getting everyone settled in their rooms. I and a man I had made friends with on the tour went out to try and secure food for everyone. It was midnight at this point and people were starving. Fortunately, we were pointed toward a restaurant that served shawarma, and they were so excited to see an Egyptian that they prepared food for fifty people and refused to accept payment for it. It was another blessing.

When we went to go pray at the mosque we discovered that because of the tensions in the area that the soldiers would not allow anyone under the age of 55 to go to the mosque to pray. I was outraged for everyone that wished to pray—all the citizens of Jerusalem who were being denied the opportunity as well as those who had traveled far to complete the tour of the three holy sites. Again, Mohamed and I were blessed. Since we were Americans there was no such restriction, and we were allowed to go and pray.

Again people made room for Mohamed and I to pray. We visited the area dedicated to the Virgin Mary, the mother of Jesus. An old man leaped up and kissed Mohamed on his forehead.

Everyone came forward to touch Mohamed. As at the other two mosques people were giving him a great deal of respect and reverence which confused me. I finally asked one man why everyone was paying so much attention to Mohamed. The man said it was because Mohamed was the future and that he was going to help change the world.

I still don't know what that means, but I did appreciate the help and care that we received throughout our trip. Jerusalem is a deeply spiritual place. You can feel the history there and the feeling of it all is amazing. It's a place that you never want to leave while at the same time you are constantly staring at your watch counting down the hours until you can get out of there. Despite its beauty and spirituality it is still a place of great conflict which makes being there uncomfortable on a different level.

When it was time to leave the area and head into Jordan there was a time crunch. There's a small checkpoint building that you have to pass through. It's out in the middle of nowhere and it closes in the early evening. Anyone not making it through has to sleep in their vehicle or on the ground until the next day. It was getting late, the place was incredibly crowded, and it was very clear not everyone was going to make it through. People were getting tense and upset and it was not a great situation. Finally, a customs official came out and told the waiting crowd that they'd be taking Americans first before anyone else. We were waving our passports in excitement as they lined us up in one area. We were so grateful to be in the group that got to go first and did our best to ignore the frustration leveled at us by the other groups. Our group made it through before the station closed and we were on our way.

The whole journey that day took so much longer than expected that I was not able to call Marim for many hours after I had been supposed to call her. She became very worried and even started calling embassies worried that something had happened. When we finally made it to our hotel in Jordan I was able to call her and let her know we were safe, much to her relief and ours.

The trip was an amazing experience, and we felt blessed and protected every step of the way. It was a wonderful experience but we were also very grateful to be able to return home and start getting back to some semblance of a normal life. Our new family was about to grow even more.

My amazing wife

11
Living the American Dream

After my daughter, Habiba, was born we settled down as a family and started trying to live a more normal life while still striving every day for the American dream. There was the usual family stuff, raising a baby, helping our son with school, working, and dealing with the expectations of family.

Every day my father would ask me when I was moving back home, and every day I would tell him that I was home, that Florida was my home. He and my mother would come to visit us, and I was able to take Marim to Egypt for her first time. That was an incredible experience getting to show her the country I had grown up in.

Marim earned her Bachelor's in Psychology. I joke that she got that degree so she can figure out what's wrong with me. I couldn't have been more proud of her and how she persevered with that even despite everything that was going on in our lives. I call her the Iron Lady because of that since she is unstoppable and so strong.

Even though I had really started to make my mark in the world of personal finance and had made good friends and loyal customers, I still encountered a lot of prejudice. It was particularly bad at one company at which I worked. I came in as the youngest manager they'd ever had. In fact, I was about twenty-five years younger than the average manager. That caused some friction with one of my coworkers who was very dismissive of me because of my age. I just kept working hard, though, and making a lot of money for my clients and the company.

Then after a while she decided to attack me because I took Friday afternoons off to go to prayers with my son just like I had been doing for years. She made out that it bothered people in the office that I got to take a half day, like I was on vacation or something. I never make anyone feel bad for their religious beliefs or needs. I never make an issue of my beliefs or anyone else's. I was furious and didn't know how to respond, but my boss's boss called me and told me that everything was going to be okay.

A few weeks later my secretary came in and informed me that my Christmas present from my boss had been delivered. I responded with enthusiasm asking what he had sent and was promptly warned that I wasn't going to like it. The man sent me a giant box filled with every pork product you can imagine from bacon to pork chops and everything in between.

I was shocked and horrified because he knew I was Muslim and could not eat pork. I took a deep breath and told myself that maybe it had just been an honest mistake. I called him up to ask him about it and discovered that it was no mistake, but a hostile gesture. I gave my two weeks' notice on the phone.

I kept finding out the hard way that not everyone is as tolerant as I am. I don't care about a person's religion, ethnicity, gender, sexual orientation, political affiliation, profession, or anything else. At the end of the day whether you're a financial planner, a grieving widower, a redneck, a nurse who loves to play Call of Duty, a drug dealer on a cross-country bus, or anyone else there are two things we all want. We want to take care of our family and live in peace. Nothing matters beyond that. That is what I teach my kids.

I moved to another company where my hard work and integrity were appreciated, and I was treated with the respect that every human being deserves. The day I was promoted to First Vice President I didn't really think much about it. Apparently, I forgot to even tell my wife about it for several weeks.

It even took me a while to realize that at some point I had actually achieved my financial goals. It was such a long journey, but my hard work, perseverance, and dedication to great service saw me through. At that moment, though, what was important to me was that I was making money for my clients, making money for my company, and making my family happy.

After all, that's what the American dream is about. It's finding your happiness and living it every day to the best of your ability despite everything else. And when life throws you a curve ball and you encounter darkness and horror, the best and greatest thing you can do is to be the light that shines and help those around you.

Letting our voices be heard

12
United We Stand

On June 12, 2016, there was a horrific slaughter at the Pulse nightclub in Orlando. Forty-nine innocent people were killed. Fifty-three were injured. It was the deadliest mass shooting in America's history. And it happened in my neighborhood.

Orlando is my home which made this particular attack all the more horrific and real to me. It happened just a short walk away from where I work. All throughout the aftermath I couldn't help but flashback repeatedly to 9/11. There was a big difference this time, though. I wasn't standing alone overseas with a group of strangers watching the events unfold. I was here, in the heart of it, watching the impact on my friends and neighbors, people I knew and cared for. Their pain was my pain. Their loss was my loss. We suffered together, and we all rallied together. I was proud to be a part of that.

It was Ramadan which meant that I was fasting. I had to do something, though. I literally just couldn't stay home and try to ignore what was happening. I went out and stood in line to give blood. It was scorching hot and I stood for hours. I was weak from the fasting, but I was determined. It was what I could do to help.

I took a picture of myself donating blood and shared it on social media, urging others to do what they could to help.

> "Yes, my name is Mahmoud, and I am a proud Muslim American. Yes, I donated blood even though I can't eat or drink anything because I'm fasting in our holy month Ramadan, just like hundreds of other Muslims who donated today here in Orlando. Yes, I'm angry for what happened last night and all the innocent lives we lost. Yes, I'm sad, frustrated and mad that a crazy guy who claimed to be a Muslim did that shameful act. Yes, I witnessed the greatness of this country, watching thousands of people standing in 92-degree sun waiting their turn to donate blood, even after they were told that the wait time was 5 to 7 hours. Yes, this is the greatest nation on earth, watching people from different ages, including kids, volunteering to give water, juice, food, umbrellas, sun block. Also, watching our old veterans coming to donate, and next to them, Muslim women in hijab carrying food and water to donors standing in line. Yes, together we will stand against hate, terrorism, extremism and racism. Yes, our blood all looks the same, so get out there

> and donate blood, because our fellow American citizens are injured and need our blood. Yes, our community in central Florida is heartbroken, but let's put our colors, religions, ethnicity, sexual orientation, and political views all aside so we can UNITE against those who are trying to hurt us."

My post quickly went viral. Before I knew it, I was being interviewed on all the major television news outlets and being written up in newspapers. I realized that I had been granted an opportunity to speak out against the hate and the violence and to urge everyone else to do the same. When we stand together, we are powerful.

It outrages me when terrorists harm innocent people and claim to be Muslim. Islam is not a religion of violence, but of peace. The Quran references both Christians and Jews as our brothers who worship the same God that we do. I cannot understand the hate. What I do understand is that it is intolerable and harms us all, no matter our religion. I also understand that when those of us who are Muslim don't speak out against it, others believe that we condone such behavior. This causes great harm both to ourselves and to our community. Silence is not an option. We must make our voices heard, and let those who perpetrate such violence know that we do not condone their behavior and do not consider them one of us.

In Orlando, following the shooting the Muslim community did just this. We spoke out. We held a rally that we called Not in Our Name where we made it clear that we despise the cowards who do these terrible acts.

I was helpless to do anything in the wake of 9/11. Now, though, I could donate blood, and speak on behalf of my community, condemning the violence, the hate, and the bloodshed.

At the rally I was proud to stand on that stage with many Muslim leaders representing 13 different organizations in central Florida. Here is the speech I gave that day:

> My fellow American citizens, dear brothers and sisters in Islam. For the past 15 years our religion has been hijacked by terrorist groups that claim they represent Islam while we all know they represent evil. For the past 15 years we as moderate Muslims have done very little to show the true face of our peaceful Islam. For the past 15 years the media has focused on Muslims and Islam in a very negative unacceptable way and more like brain washing to our fellow American citizens. Their job was easy for them since, on one hand, we have those terrorist attacks intensifying across the globe, and it's getting worse while, on the other hand, we, the vast majority, the

99.9% of Muslims, have been quiet, defensive with very little and passive response.

For the past 15 years the voice of bullets have been louder than the voice of our holy Quran. For the past 15 years the images of bombing , killing and destruction across the globe have been widely shared versus the images of unity and peace.

But we are here today to say enough is enough. We are here today to send a very loud and clear message to all those terrorist groups which are anti-American, anti-Islam, anti-human, anti-peace and all their followers, supporters or even [those who] have sympathy for those killers, not just in our beloved America, but across the whole world.

As American Muslims we all stand for Peace. American Muslims stand against Terrorism. American Muslims stand against Hate. And when we say hate we are talking about all different forms of hate and against any US citizen. Hate against different minorities like our central Florida LGBT which cost us 49 innocent victims, hate against African-

Americans and the attacks in their churches or individuals like the case of Castile, hate against Latinos, hate against women, hate against our men & women in uniform like the 5 officers in Dallas, hate against us Muslims here in the U.S. from personal attacks to hate messages on mosques' walls.

We are tired of… paying the price twice for every incident that happens. We get the pain of seeing our country and fellow American citizens under attack and also we get to fear for our families and friends' safety worrying about backlash for a crime that we didn't do or support but was done in our name and the name of Islam.

We know what terrorism is like. Just in the holy month of Ramadan several Muslim countries were attacked from Istanbul to Baghdad and from Bangladesh to Our prophet Mohamed "peace be on him" Holy Medina. Hundreds of our innocent Muslim brothers and sisters lost their lives; they were shopping for Eid cloth and ended up shopping for their coffins.

From Syria to Libya and from Yemen to Lebanon, from Tunisia to Algeria and Pakistan to India. Sunni, Shite, Aloui, Durzi, Ismailis.We as Muslims [have] paid the biggest price tag of terrorism. We lost millions of lives to that black, new, unknown, bloody, unjust, inhuman, brutal act called terror [at] the hands of [a] few crazy, blood suckers--insane individuals who claim to be Muslims and they have nothing to do with Islam.

That's why our event name is “Not In My Name.”

So, when we have a crazy, insane, lunatic individual attacking other peaceful innocent civilians we tell this coward.

[Crowd shouted “Not in my name!”]

When we have a group claiming they represent Islam with black flags and blood on their hands we say to those killers.

[Crowd shouted “Not in my name!”]

When we have the media trying to paint all 1.6 billion Muslims in general and especially American Muslims as bad guys we say to them.

[Crowd shouted “Not in my name!”]

When someone chants Allah Akbar while he is getting ready to take the lives of those who were created by God, we tell that animal.

[Crowd shouted “Not in my name!”]

We are not here to be apologetic because we haven't done anything wrong. Actually, Muslim Americans for over 400 years have been a very active and positive part of the American fabric with remarkable contributions in many different fields from medicine to accounting and from space to serving in the armed forces of the USA.

We are here to stand with all our friends and families in the USA, to stand with our friends in the LGBT, African American, Women rights, Latino, Christian, Jewish, Indian, Arab, Middle East communities hand-in-hand for our generation and our children’s future generation, we are here to say only love will conquer hate. Only United we will

> win but divided we will fail. That it's time to put our differences aside and unite against those who are trying to hurt us, who are trying to divide us, who are trying to make us turn on each other.
>
> It's time to realize that no matter what is our religion, background, ethnicity, sexual orientation, political views, gender at the end of the day, we are all humans--sons and daughters of Adam and Eve with the same blood running in our veins. This is the time we need to take down the walls of hate and build bridges of love and peace.
>
> God bless all Americans and God bless the United States of America.

It has been said that for the only thing required for evil to prevail is for good men to do nothing. I refuse to do nothing. I am proud to stand up and be a voice of reason and compassion. I am proud to be an American patriot and I will do what I can to let others know that and to teach others about the true Islam and to teach future generations of Muslims that love is always stronger than hate.

The family on Wall Street

13
The Future

Life goes on. Orlando has been healing since the tragedy that struck our community. My family continues to give blood regularly. After so many gave blood for us when Mohamed was in the hospital, how can we not?

I always encourage people to do what they can to make a difference in the lives of those around them. Donate blood, volunteer your time, help educate people and do what you can to ease another's burden. Go the extra mile for your friends, families, clients, and, yes, even strangers.

I have achieved my American dream, but the journey doesn't end here. The journey continues onward. That is the wonderful thing about this particular journey. There is always a new goal, a new dream beckoning. We can set our sights on financial independence, the freedom to do what we want when we want to. We can also set our sights on the dream of making this a better country and a better world for all.

I know that for sure we all have to work together to achieve the dream we all have—liberty and justice for all. I dream of the day that my son doesn't have to worry that his name is Mohamed, that my neighbor doesn't have to worry about his color, and that my female coworkers don't have to worry about pay discrimination. I long for the time when all humans get to enjoy our planet earth as a home to all of us regardless of our ethnicities, religions, colors, gender, sexual orientation, or nationalities. I challenge anyone to show me that they have a different color blood than the rest of us. We are all sick of wars, violence, hate, inequality, injustice and being judged.

I dream of the day that people stop treating each other based on materiel things like their physical looks or weight or even their names. I dream of the day that we get to choose what we want to be without worrying about failure or social status. I dream of a cure to cancer so there can be an end to the disease that is taking human lives all over the world. I dream of the day that the world is one big home and everyone gets to travel without visas or fear that they will be rejected. I dream that all the kids of the world get to enjoy their future without worrying about the current political status. I dream that we stop calling each other names based on things we didn't get to choose like our countries of origin or our skin colors. I dream that we all have equal opportunities to achieve our dreams without struggles or fighting for our God-given rights.

I know that is a lot to dream, but I also know there are many people who have the same dream. All these dreams can be achieved if we put our differences behind us and focus on things that we all have in common.

We all bleed the same color. We all want to take care of our families. We want to pursue happiness and have the freedom to live life as we choose. We all want to live in peace.

You cannot imagine how hard I worked to be called an American. America was founded on the principle that all men are created equal. I believe in that. I believe that almost every American believes in that. It's time to start acting like that and lead by example, not just for our children but also for the children of the world. Life is a journey that will end, and I made a promise to be remembered that I came and left in peace.

About the Authors

Mahmoud ElAwadi is a proud Egyptian-American who immigrated to the United States fifteen years ago to start from the bottom in order to reach the top. Well-known in many financial circles he was catapulted into the public eye in the days following the shooting at the Orlando Pulse Nightclub. He has since been active in helping others understand Muslims and helping Muslims find their voice to speak out against violence perpetrated by anyone. He believes deeply that part of the American dream is freedom for all to be themselves and not to be chained by old ideas, stereotypes, and prejudices.

Debbie Viguié is the New York Times Bestselling author of fifty novels. Debbie writes mysteries and thrillers including the Psalm 23 Mysteries and Witch Hunt series both of which are currently being considered for development for television. She writes the Tex Ravencroft science fiction adventure series with her husband, Dr. Scott Viguié. In addition to her other pursuits she also ghostwrites memoirs and self-help books for leaders in many fields. Visit her online at: www.debbieviguie.com.

Made in the USA
Middletown, DE
19 November 2018